N ederlands
letterenfonds
dutch foundation
for literature

This publication has been made possible with financial support
from the Dutch Foundation for Literature.

First published in the United States, Great Britain, Canada, Australia, and New Zealand in 2018
by NorthSouth Books, Inc., an imprint of NordSüd Verlag AG, CH-8050 Zürich, Switzerland.

Distributed in the United States by NorthSouth Books, Inc., New York 10016.
Library of Congress Cataloging-in-Publication Data is available.

ISBN: 978-0-7358-4314-1 (trade edition)

1 3 5 7 9 · 10 8 6 4 2

Printed in China 2017

www.northsouth.com

for Audrey with love

Audrey Hepburn and Givenchy

BY PHILIP HOPMAN

North South

Hubert's mother was giving yet another party. The chateau (castle) was decorated with a thousand red roses. The guests were drinking champagne, dancing, and flirting.

Audrey lived in a different castle. "Mama," said Audrey, "I will be a ballet dancer someday."

Hubert did not like dancing, but he was in awe of
the beautiful dresses.

"That's great, darling, " her mother replied.

"Mama, I will be a fashion designer someday," Hubert said.

"You will never become a great ballerina, dear," said Audrey's ballet teacher.

"That's just fine, cheri," replied his mother. "Will you make me something beautiful too?"

"Your feet are too big and you're a tad too long."

Clothing these days is much too complicated, thought Hubert. *They could be a lot simpler and more elegant.*

Audrey wanted more. But no more ballet. She decided to move to London and take acting classes.

He designed the most beautiful dresses. Dashing loose blouses and skirts to match. And a fun little hat to top it off.

Soon after, Audrey was in the spotlight. She took her first steps into her movie career and the magazines instantly adored her.

Hubert's very first fashion show was a gigantic success. People had not seen such fresh designs before in Paris!

All the ladies wanted Hubert's dresses, jackets, and blouses. Especially the Bettina blouse, which was white with black trim. It was a sensation!

Audrey got her first big film offer. She was to play a princess who got tired of being a princess and ran off. Her costar was incredibly handsome, and famous as well.

Soon, all the famous ladies wanted a dress by Hubert.

Audrey needed clothes for her next movie. But everything she tried was stupid.

Actresses, opera singers, princesses, and even the first lady.

Too wide, too colorful, too fancy, too old-fashioned, or just plain ugly.

Meanwhile, Hubert was increasingly busy. Orders kept rolling in, and he was working hard on a new collection.

"Maybe you ought to visit that hip designer, that Hubert de . . . what's his name?" mentioned Audrey's friend.

"Today a young actress will visit you," his assistant, Philippe, told him.
"A certain Miss Hepburn."

Audrey flew to Paris to visit Hubert's studio. First she cut off her ponytail.

"Hubert, this is Audrey," Philippe said. "Audrey, this is Hubert."

"Nice to meet you, mademoiselle," Hubert said. "You need clothes for a movie? I'm afraid I have no time to design anything.

"But you are welcome to see what's on the rack."
Audrey tried the clothes, and they were a perfect fit.
"As if I made them for you," Hubert said.

In her next movie, Audrey played a frivolous woman who liked having breakfast

at a jewelry store! The dresses that Hubert designed for her were unforgettable.

Audrey was now world famous. All the girls wanted to wear
the cute outfits that Audrey wore in the movie.

And even some boys.

Audrey had a glamorous life. Meanwhile, she traveled the world to raise awareness for children in need. She always wore Hubert's clothes. Even when she baked chocolate cake.

"Is that Hubert your boyfriend?" friends would ask Audrey.

"Oh no," she answered. "He is much more than that. When I wear his clothes, I feel safe. I'm not afraid of anything."

"Hi Audrey, Hubert here. Where are you? In Africa again?
Are you taking good care of yourself?
Oh, I'm doing great. I just went for a walk.

"The garden is so beautiful now. Wish you were here too.
Will I see you soon?"

"Hubert, will we be friends forever?"

"Yes, Audrey. Forever."